The Best Romantic Ideas

for Every Day of the Year

365
Great Ways to Say
I Love You

Mara Goodman-Davies

SOURCEBOOKS CASABLANCA™
AN IMPRINT OF SOURCEBOOKS, INC.®
NAPERVILLE, ILLINOIS

Published by Casablanca, an imprint of Sourcebooks, Inc.
P.O. Box 4410, Naperville, Illinois 60567-4410
(630) 961-3900
Fax: (630) 961-2168
www.sourcebooks.com
ISBN-13: 978-1-4022-0811-9
ISBN-10: 1-4022-0811-1

Printed and bound in Canada
TR 10 9 8 7 6 5 4 3 2 1

Table of Contents

A Daily Dose of Romance:

Ideas for Anytime

The Basics of Love

1. All You Need Is Love

- Look your lover straight in the eyes and say, "I love you."
- Call each other once a day from work just to say "I love you."
- Drink a glass of champagne. Toast your lovely partnership.

2. Love's Sweet Kiss

- Kiss each other first thing every morning and last thing every night.
- Sneak a few kisses when you're in public.
- Kiss your lover's eyebrows.
- Kiss your lover's eyelashes.

3. Playful Love

- Nibble on your lover's earlobes.
- Blow in your lover's ear.
- Rub noses.
- Give each other "butterfly kisses" with your eyelashes.

4. Sexy Acts of Love

- Wear as little as possible.
- Brush each other's hair.
- Make love in broad daylight.
- Get in the hot tub.
- When you leave for work or do chores in the morning, make sure you both have on one piece of sexy lingerie underneath your functional clothing. It will give you each something to think about all day!

5. Sensuous and Sensual

- Try a body-to-body massage using massage oil or baby oil. If this does not get your partner in the mood for love, nothing will!
- Buy the *Kama Sutra*, an Indian book of love, romance, and sex. This is the ultimate guide to pleasure on a mental, physical, emotional, and spiritual level.

6. Five Tests of Love's Endurance

- Kiss for at least fifteen seconds in the morning.
- Kiss for at least fifteen seconds when you first see each other after work.
- Stay up all night.
- See how long you can kiss without coming up for air.
- See how far you can walk while giving each other piggyback rides.

A Day in the Love of...

7. Wake Up with Your Lover

- Wake your lover up with a few romantic lines from *Romeo and Juliet*.
- Feed each other breakfast.
- Wake up at dawn together and watch the sunrise.
- Make a romantic wish for the day.

8. Love Throughout the Day

- End every sentence you say to your lover with "I love you" for one whole day.
- Hold hands wherever you go.
- Smile all day.

9. At the End of the Day

- Spend a cozy night sipping wine together.
- Watch the sunset together.
- Make a date to have a private cocktail party together at dinnertime.

10. In the Name of Love

- Make up new nicknames for each other.
- Get matching personalized license plates.

The History and Mystery of Love Revealed

11. Humble Beginnings of Love

- Frame both your baby pictures together.
- Trace each other's family history or do a family tree. By climbing each other's family tree, you can have fun learning about all the people who helped make your lover the person he is today.
- Get out some old high school year-books or family albums that will take you and your lover on a romantic trip down memory lane.

12. Love's Fondest Memories

- Take turns telling some of the funny stories that you share together.
- Take some time to talk about things you haven't discussed in awhile. Reclaim your love for one another.

- Take turns retelling some of the romantic times you've had.

13. The Mysteries of Love Revealed

- Tell each other secrets.
- Interview each other with ten questions you have about your pasts, <u>preferences</u>, and <u>experiences</u>. When you are finished, you will have a more intimate love and appreciation for each other.

The Traditions of Love

14. Customs for You and Your Lover

- Since spring is a time of rebirth and renewal, <u>make spring resolutions to improve your life</u> and your love.
- Assign each other a personal gemstone.
- Assign each other a personal flower.
- Assign each other a personal day of the week.
- Assign each other a personal color.

15. Bedtime Rituals

- Read Shakespearean sonnets to one another before bed.
- Tell your lover a romantic bedtime story.
- Both you and your partner choose your favorite book. Take turns reading a chapter aloud to one another before bed.

Fun with Love

16. Love and Games

- Challenge each other to speak in an English accent. The first one who slips up or forgets has to read a Shakespearean sonnet five times in a row.
- Do a jigsaw, crossword, or sudoku puzzle together.
- Learn a magic trick.
- Take turns being each other's personal slave for a day.

17. Fun with Food
- Eat hot dogs. Write each other's name with mustard.
- Share a bowl of pasta. Eat each string starting at opposite ends until your lips meet.
- Feed each other honey off a spoon.
- Have a spontaneous food fight.

18. Nothing Like a Good Joke
- Call her at work and say that she's won the lottery—the lottery of love, that is! Make up a prize.
- Replace the beer bottles and potato chips with champagne and strawberries.
- Replace the favorite CDs in his car with romantic music.

19. Playful and in Love
- Have a tickle contest.
- Giggle together.
- Play footsie.
- Have a pillow fight.
- Whisper sweet nothings.

Learning about Love

20. The Language of Love
- Make up your own sign language and be sure that you are the only ones who understand the messages of love your hands convey to each other.
- Learn how to say "I love you" in five new languages.
- Learn to speak Italian, the most romantic of the Romance languages, together.

21. Get Creative
Sign up for an art class together. Developing your artistic talents will help you and your lover enjoy a wealth of uninhibited expression.

Tokens of Love

22. Put It on a List

- Make a list of romantic things that you two would like to do for or with each other.
- Make a list of the ten things you love most about your lover.
- Write down the top ten romantic things to do that you've always dreamed of doing but never had the time. After both your lists are complete, pick one!

23. Surprise Tokens of Affection

- Leave a sweet note in his briefcase.
- Grab a stick or fallen branch and write your names in the snow, encircled by a big heart. Make sure she can't miss it on her way out of the house in the morning!
- Put a cup of hot coffee in the car's drink holder with a donut. Write "I love you" on the napkin.
- Leave a rose on the car seat.

24. Leave Your Troubles Behind

- Give each other a break from any negative issues, arguments, or discussion that you may be working through for one day.
- Make a list of all your exes and burn them in a ceremonial bonfire together.
- Do one really great thing for each other to make up for all the not-so-nice things you might have done during the year.

Your Lover,
Your Favorite Celebrity

25. And the Oscar Goes to...
- Thank your lover for treating you and making you feel like a celebrity every day.
- Tell your lover that he will always be the star of your show.
- Tell your lover that only the best is good enough for her.

Four Anytime Love Notes
Every day is full of opportunities to say "I love you" with a quick note left in an unexpected—or favorite—spot.

26. Love for Breakfast
- "I could live on our love alone" on the refrigerator.

- "Your love melts my heart" in the freezer.
- "I'm so glad we're playing on the same team" in the sports section of the newspaper.

27. Thinking of You All Day Long

- "Our love is wealth beyond measure" in a wallet.
- "Your love feeds my heart and nourishes my soul" in a lunch bag.
- "You've got me in your pocket" in the pocket of a shirt or coat.

28. Love on the Road

- "You drive me wild" on the car steering wheel.
- "I want to travel with you down the highway of life" on the passenger seat.
- "You are my favorite hot rod" on the door of the garage.

29. The Melody of Love

- "Our love is the music of my life" on the stereo.
- "You sing the songs of my heart" on a CD case.
- "You make love like a rock star" on the radio.

The Great Indoors:

Making the Sparks Fly at Home

Love's Décor

30. The next time you and your lover see a tag sale, take a minute and start picking! You can find items in a garage sale that have romantic personal flair.

31. Go to an art exhibition that features only the works of new artists. If you can afford it, buy a piece of new art together and keep it as an investment. That way, if the artist becomes famous, you can say you knew him when.

32. Redecorate your house together. Fixing up the place you live with your lover can be very romantic because it appeals to your nesting instincts.

33. Love in Bloom

- Enjoy picking beautiful flowers from your own garden or go to a local nursery for potted blooms. Make lovely, colorful bouquets for your dining room, bedroom, and bathrooms. The arrival of fresh spring flowers in the house always creates a soft, romantic environment. It's like having a constant reminder of new love everywhere you turn.
- Fill your bedroom with flowers.
- Leave a bouquet of roses on the breakfast table.

Love's Kitchen

34. Gourmet Love

- Cook lobster together for a wonderful meal at home.
- Serve a sexy dessert wine with a simple meal.

- Learn how to make your lover's favorite dish. Surprise her with a home-cooked gourmet meal.
- After picking fresh fruits or vegetables, make some heartwarming dishes together starring your pick of the day.

35. Meals Cooked with Love

- Once the weather has changed for the better, it's time to get outside and grill that killer rack of ribs you've been boasting about all spring. Share your favorite summertime memories together.
- Cook brunch together.
- Make a big salad together.

36. Baking with Your Lover

- Make French bread together.
- Knead bread or pizza crust together.

- Bake a pie, cake, or cookies.
  Lick the spoon together.

37. **Five Dinner Dates at Home**
- Dine on leftovers by candlelight.
- Have an intimate dinner party for two.
- Have breakfast very early by candlelight.
- Have a picnic on the living room floor.
- Have a barbecue in bed. Get a big towel and spread it across your covers. Lay the food out on the bed and get naked, except for some cowboy hats and boots (if you have them), or just wear plastic bibs.

Signs of Love's Cleansing Power

38. **Good Clean Fun**
- Surprise your lover with a rose in the shower.

- Give your lover a bubble bath and scrub every inch of him.
- Take a shower together.
- Write a quote from a Shakespearean love sonnet on the bathroom mirror in shaving cream.

39. Fill your bathtub with water and add cinnamon and rose oil. Float some gardenia flowers on top if possible, or get yourself gardenia-scented bubble bath. Ease into the soothing water together and savor the scents of the oils and flowers.

Hocus Pocus

40. Love's Essential Oils

Create your own love oil. Start with almond, sesame, or baby oil as a base. Add some of your favorite aromatherapy essential oils. Focus on your most romantic feelings while you make your aphrodisiac. Before you and your lover share a night of passion, anoint yourself with a little dab of your special oil on your wrists, on the nape of your neck, or anywhere else, and ignite some magic sparks between the two of you.

41. Ritual Love

- Go to the park and write your lover's name in pebbles or branches.
- Throw a penny or a pebble into a brook and make three romantic wishes or declarations of love.
- Make marshmallow and raisin figures of you and your lover, then roast them together on a stick.
- Carve both of your names and birthdays into a big, red candle. Let it burn out.

42. Sometimes Love Means Staying Home

Take a day of rest and relaxation together. Postpone the errands and spend the day puttering around the garden or lazing together in bed.

Labors of Love

43. Weekend Warriors

- Paint your house (or a room) together.
- Wash the windows together.
- To make the household chores go swiftly and painlessly, put on some fun music while you sweep, pack, and scrub, and take lots of breaks to smile at and kiss each other.

44. Entrust your lover with the task of cleaning out your side of the closet, while he entrusts you with cleaning out his. You will learn a lot about each other's likes and dislikes, as well as

personal tastes. There are bound to be artifacts that will give you both a good laugh or revive some romantic memories of times past.

Romantic Adventures at Home

45. Return to those happy-go-lucky summertime days by turning your home into a summer camp together. Tell one another your camp love stories.

46. Get out your tent and sleeping bags and set them up in the living room. Strategically place stuffed animals around the room and get a CD of rainforest sounds. You and your lover can pretend that you just came back to camp after a day in the bush and are ripe for a night in the wild!

47. Love Makes a House a Home
- Start a fire in the fireplace.
- Wear your oldest sweats and cuddle up on the couch.
- Explore the attic.
- Look for a lost item together.
- Ask your lover to carry you across the threshold of your front door every day for a week.

48. A Haven for Lovers
- Take turns modeling nude for one another, using various furniture and household items as props.
- Make a sexy video in the comfort of your own home.
- Leave rose petals on the bed.
- Begin to strip the minute you walk in the door.
- Take pictures of your lover posing in sexy lingerie or sitting in the bath

surrounded by bubbles. Later on, make a collage of your pictures and put them in a secret book or paste them up on a big piece of cardboard.

A Spa of Love

49. Cover your bodies from head to toe in a mud mask that you can find at any beauty counter in a department store. Take advantage of summer weather by pulling out some lounge chairs and letting the sun bake the mud. Have a playful time washing each other off with a garden hose.

50. Slather moisturizing foot lotion on each other and wrap all four of your feet together in a warm towel. Playing footsie with slippery, creamy feet can quickly become a tickling session!

51. Treat yourselves to a full-body wrap. Choose a lively, fragrant lotion (preferably with aloe) and heat it up in the microwave. Cover yourself and your lover in the hot lotion, spreading it on from head to toe. Meanwhile, dampen some huge bath towels or bed sheets in warm water. When the towels are ready, wrap yourself and your lover together in the towels and lie down on the bed. Experience the joy of intimacy as your bodies soak up the healing treatment.

52. Facing Love Together
Try giving each other a soothing facial. You can do this with products containing essential oils like eucalyptus and green tea for stimulation, or lavender and chamomile for calming and toning.

57. Ylang Ylang helps you rekindle those infatuated, flirtatious feelings of new love, and promotes a healthy fantasy break from daily routines. If you and your lover are feeling bored, or are looking for a diversion from the everyday, Ylang Ylang will add some spice to your relationship!

58. Grapefruit makes you sharp, witty, and ready for anything. After a grapefruit massage, you and your lover will feel spry, agile, and bursting with energy. This sharp citrus scent will give you both the boost you need to embark on a grand, romantic adventure.

59. Clary sage promotes expansiveness and clear thinking and helps lovers widen their horizons. If your relationship is in a rut, it will help you both to think outside the box and come up with some new ideas for romance.

60. Basil can fortify a romance by helping each of you honor and respect your own identity first, giving you room to honor and respect your partner. Not just for spaghetti sauce, the scent of this herb will help you to grow as individuals while also nurturing your relationship.

61. Peppermint is a great uplifter. It can give new life to tired, achy muscles. Give one another a vigorous massage using peppermint oil. Allow your lover's hands to ease any tension you are feeling as the scent of the oil rejuvenates you.

62. Jasmine is an exotic aphrodisiac that promotes extravagant fantasies, boundless creativity, and intensified perception. This scent provides a perfect segue into a round of role-playing, which will make you feel youthful and brazen.

63. Orange oil will make you feel light, friendly, and open. An orange oil massage can make you and your lover feel bright and sunny all over. Let the citrus scent invigorate your senses and get you ready for a night of love!

64. Patchouli oil can help you get a good night's rest. It can also be an aphrodisiac, in a warm and fuzzy, comfortable way. If you are feeling low on energy, but wish to enjoy a quiet evening at home with your partner, some patchouli oil will set the mood for a romantic night of cuddling in front of the fireplace.

65. Lemon inspires lovers to keep a positive attitude. A hot lemon oil massage is great for romantic healing. If you find yourself complaining after a long day at work or about life's various quirks, heat up some lemon oil and bring your attention back where it belongs—on your lover.

66. Mandarin helps soften the rough edges of your day and returns you to a gentle, carefree state of being. It will lighten your hearts and relieve your frustrations. Use this sweet scent to ease your nerves after an argument. Soon, you will forget why you were fighting in the first place!

67. Rubbing pine oil on the soles of your feet and between your toes will uplift you and give you boundless energy. Give your lover a vigorous foot massage with the oil and generate enough energy for some unforgettable passion.

68. Chamomile's greatest quality is its ability to soothe. Use this essential oil to make the world right again. This is the perfect scent to clear your mind after an argument or if you are facing a big decision together. It will give you the peace of mind you need to move forward together.

69. Juniper causes great expansion of the mind, body, and soul. If you are both looking to try new things or go on an exotic trip together, but need an extra boost to give you courage, juniper's bold scent will propel you to romantic greatness!

70. Sandalwood reconnects lovers with their personal power and sense of attractiveness, making love a more con-nected and richer experience. Its strong scent will make you both feel as if you are on top the world and will reaffirm the wonderful connection the two of you share. Light a sandalwood-scented candle tonight and rediscover the attraction that brought you together in the beginning.

71. Ginger has wonderful healing qualities and has also been known to enhance memory. Ginger brings warmth and opening to your body

and soul. Allow the root's sweet scent to open up your memory and help you to remember all the little things that have defined your relationship. Take turns recounting all of the little incidents and details that have made your relationship so fulfilling.

72. A shameless aphrodisiac that can get anyone in the mood for love, rose oil is also known for potent healing powers that inspire the user with visions of beauty and love. This scent is a romantic staple that is sure to have you spouting sonnets or serenading your lover.

73. Tangerine will help open you to new, fresh perspectives. It will put the smiles back on your faces and make you feel like summer inside and out. If one of you is looking to change careers or embark on a new project, tangerine is the perfect scent to

inspire you and open your mind to new possibilities.

Love's Playground

74. Pretend that you are Roman lovers. Wrap sheets around you to make togas. Decorate your heads with leaves. Have your lover sit in a chair and pretend that he is the Emperor of Rome. Feed him grapes from the vine. When the last one is gone, enjoy a safe Roman orgy!

75. Have your lover dress up as a butler and have him bring you sandwiches, pastries, strawberries, and whipped cream. If you are happy with his service, invite him to join you. Order your servant to nibble on your neck and earlobes and blow in your ear seductively. If he carries out your orders to your satisfaction,

show him how much you appreciate his devoted servitude!

76. Prepare a feast for King Arthur and his Round Table! When you are done eating, put on an ethereal CD and do a little dance. Finish up your dance by curtsying to the ground and having him escort you into the bedroom for a night of love with your knight in shining armor.

77. Dress as a French maid and make sure to have at least one piece of sexy lingerie on underneath. Turn down the bed and unpack his things. Next, bring in a tray of cheeses, crackers, chocolates, and wine. Ask your lover if there is anything you can do to make his stay more enjoyable. Tell him that if he doesn't have his every whim catered to, you will lose your job.

78. Turn your own home into a James Bond romantic hideaway. Your lover should pretend that he is James Bond and use a flashlight to search the house for bad guys. When the coast is clear, bring out piping-hot pots of chocolate and cheese fondue. Dip bits of bread and strawberries into them and feed each other seductively. Make love like two world-class, sophisticated people of intrigue.

79. The Spanish tango has often been called the dance of love—a very romantic thing to do around your house when it is chilly outside. It is even more romantic if you strip while you tango. Every time there is a pause in the music, take one article of clothing off of each other until you are both totally naked. Keep dancing around until you find yourselves tangoing right into the bedroom!

80. The bullfight is a very romantic
Spanish tradition. Decide which one
of you is going to be the matador
and which one of you is going to be
the bull. You and your lover will find
yourselves spinning around the
room again and again, until you col-
lapse with passionate laughter.

81. The fan has been a crucial tool in
the romantic courting process in
many cultures. Do a fan dance for
your lover. Turn off all the lights
and prepare a Spanish-themed
meal. Have a trail of candles leading
to the bedroom and Spanish music
playing in the background. Using a
shawl and a fan, do a very seductive
dance for your lover that lets him
know how much you want him.

It's Party Time:

There's Always an Excuse to Celebrate Love

Valentine's Day

82. No matter how much your lover swears up and down that a singing telegram will be too embarrassing, there is bound to be a romantic thrill when the guy in the Cupid suit shows up at the office. There will be no doubt in anybody's mind that your partner is the one with the hot love life!

83. Find a spa in your area that gives couples massages.

84. Call a skywriting service and set up a time with the pilot to fly over your house with a message of love.

85. Hire a chef or culinary-arts student to prepare a special meal for you and your lover.

86. Hide your panties somewhere in the car where he would least expect to find them.

87. If your schedule allows it, pop down to see your lover at lunchtime for a quickie.

88. Send a chauffeur to pick your lover up at work in a limo or fancy car complete with a bar, hors d'oeuvres, and you!

89. Send a personal assistant or cleaning crew to your lover for the day to do annoying chores around the house. Also, send a makeup artist, massage therapist, manicurist, and hairdresser to the house throughout the day. She will love being catered to, even if it's just for one magical day!

90. Spending Valentine's Day night in a hotel can be a romantic adventure. Sleeping under a different roof can make you feel as though you were on a mini-vacation. You and your lover will want to make the most of this night of decadence!

91. Serenade your lover outside the bedroom window. Remember, this is a testament of love, not an audition, so don't worry if you were kicked out of the chorus as a kid.

Red, Red Wine

What follows is a list of wines to complement your relationship. Read about the twenty-three different types of grapes and what they mean to you and your lover!

92. **Barbera**: an earthy, robust grape that can bring out the barbarian in you. Drink it slowly, and even the most timid will discover the wild thing within!

93. **Cabernet Franc**: creating a taste that is both sweet and herbaceous, these soft grapes will put the spring back into your step—and make you get all kissy-face with the one you love.

94. **Cabernet Sauvignon**: if you are involved in a royal romance, these are the crème de la crème of rich, regal grapes. After a glass or two, you will feel powerful and in control.

95. **Chardonnay**: these potent grapes produce a rich, almost creamy taste combined with a fruity simplicity that will make you feel like snuggling and cuddling.

96. **Chenin Blanc**: these grapes will put you in a carefree, laid back, anything goes mood. For some easy, smooth drinking, Chenin Blanc is perfect for an afternoon barbecue or dining al fresco.

97. **Gamay**: the young, fruity, and whimsical taste of these grapes is known to make even the most mature lovers feel like kids again. This is a great wine when you and your lover need an evening of light-hearted love and affection.

98. **Garnacha:** a seduction secret of the Spanish for many centuries, these grapes have the flair of Latin love and Flamenco flaming passion. They can add a little mystery to any romance from Madrid to Minneapolis.

99. **Melon:** because of its dry, direct taste, you and your lover may find yourselves reading *War and Peace* together, or having a cerebral conversation about the origin of life.

100. **Merlot:** these rotund, chubby little grapes will make you feel warm and fuzzy inside. Grab your lover like a much loved teddy bear and show him how to heat up a nippy fall evening.

101. **Muller-Thurgau:** if you are a simple, no-frills minimalist at heart, then you will enjoy a glass of wine made with these grapes. This is for lovers who take themselves very seriously!

102. **Nebbiolo**: think pizza and lasagna—these Italian homegrown goodies will make you and your lover become absolutely *Moonstruck*. That's amoré!

103. **Petite Syrah**: these left-coast crazies will have you and your lover California dreamin' in no time. They produce rich, deep glasses of intense, romantic wine.

104. **Pinot Blanc**: these grapes are a favorite in France for making fun, fruity, and often flirty glasses of the white stuff. They are great for a casual come on or a lover's languid liaison.

105. **Pinot Noir**: grown in cool, crisp climates, these grapes produce soft, subtle wine that can make a fall evening feel like summer all over again.

106. **Riesling**: you and your lover will adore the fruity, fragrant bouquet of Riesling grapes. A bottle of this wine will make you feel like you are standing in a field of your favorite flowers.

107. **Sangiovese**: a down-home, hearty type of grape that makes a meaty glass of wine. Watch out—it is known to bring out the lusty peasant in the most proper princess!

108. **Sauvignon Blanc:** for lovers who are in the mood for a stress-free day outdoors, these grapes make the wine for sporty types. Great with food, sauvignon blanc is perfect for a picnic in the park when you decide to give your relationship a rest!

109. **Semillon:** when you're ready for romance, these grapes create a glass of wine that tells your lover you are so ripe you should be tasted before you fall from the tree.

110. **Shiraz:** if underneath your business suit you are a saucy little tart at heart, then these are the grapes for the shameless hussy in you.

111. **Sylvander:** don't have a big budget for a night of wining and dining? Have no fear—Sylvander grapes make a wine that will give you and your lover a night of affordable affection.

112. **Syrah**: unlike the Petite Syrah, this rambunctious, robust bunch of black grapes makes a glass of wine that demands your full respect and attention.

113. **Temprillo**: like a temptress from the land of macho matadors and raging bulls, these grapes have Spanish eyes that can work as a sexy aphrodisiac.

114. **Zinfandel**: this native son good ol' boy grape makes a wine that is unique to American soil. When you and your lover feel passionately patriotic, a bottle of Zinfandel at your Thanksgiving meal will make you swoon.

New Year's in Love

115. Add an aura of romance and elegance to your New Year's Eve by going on a chartered cruise.

116. Don't feel obligated to do something extravagant on New Year's Eve. Staying home and being comfy on the biggest party night of the year tells the world all you two need is love.

117. Host an intimate couples dinner party on New Year's Eve (or brunch the next day). Ask a partner in each couple to stand up and tell the story of how they met and one romantic resolution for the new year. A night like this will certainly put all who participate in the mood for love.

Five New Holidays to Show Your Love

118. Celebrate Favorite Color Day together. Wear your lover's favorite color, buy gifts in that color, and make a colorful dessert. The sky is the limit!

119. Celebrate Favorite Music Day. Surround your lover with his favorite singer or band.

120. Celebrate Favorite Food Day. Indulge your lover by providing his or her favorite food throughout the day.

121. Celebrate Favorite Movie Day. Create a "live in your favorite movie" day and let your lover live out his or her fantasies.

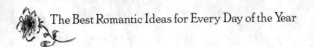

122. Celebrate *This Is Your Life* Day. Find movies from her childhood, make her favorite breakfast, play her favorite high school music, and unearth some of her favorite childhood toys.

123. Love Renewed

Plan a romantic recommitment ceremony. You and your lover can have a big party and invite all your friends to witness this lovely occasion or just privately sneak off to a romantic location. No matter how you choose to do it, expressing to each other your feelings of love is always a very special way of reminding the world—and each other—how much you love one another.

124. Halloween Feast

Cook your lover's favorite meal. Set the table in your best romantic fashion and write a menu carefully on parchment paper with a calligraphy pen. Pour wine into goblets and drink it with your arms intertwined. Savor the meal you have prepared for your lover, watching the glow of candlelight reflecting in his eyes.

Christmas

125. On the day after Thanksgiving, go to the store and buy enough candy canes for each day until Christmas. Every morning, leave your lover a candy cane with a Post-it® note counting down how many days left until December 25th. Write "I Love You" on the note.

126. If you've bought your lover a special gift this year for Christmas, intensify the surprise by dropping little hints two or three weeks before the big day. Your lover will know that something great is coming but won't be able to guess what it is!

127. Buying a Christmas tree is a wonderfully romantic ritual for couples. If you live in an area where you can go chop down your own tree, this will add warmth and depth to what has lately become a very manufactured holiday.

128. Trimming the tree and putting up the tacky holiday décor can be very romantic. While you are hanging lights and sipping eggnog, share stories and childhood memories about what you like and dislike most about the holiday season. Make your own ornaments to hang on the tree or a romantic star with your names inside

a big heart to top the tree. The holiday season should be a testament to
the love you share all year long.

129. Write down all the romantic things
that you wish your lover would do
for you on little slips of paper and
put them in a box or jar. Have him
do the same in a separate box or
jar. On Christmas Day, shake up
each other's jars and then pick one.

130. Go couple caroling together. Lock
arms with your lover and go from
house to house, spreading love and
good cheer.

131. Go to Midnight Mass together on Christmas Eve, even if you are not Catholic. The spiritual message for peace and love to all mankind can be appreciated by people of all religions during this time of year.

132. Kiss under the mistletoe.

From the Heart:

Love Letters, Gifts, and Treats

Literary Love

133. The Book of Love

- Write a series of novellas placing you and your lover in dangerously romantic situations around the world.
- Get her to tell you her most painful memory, and then rewrite it with a happy ending.
- Write the story of how you first met.

134. Love Poetry

- Write your own love sonnet.
- Write a poem about why she is so important to you and why she is the best lover in the whole world!
- Write a minimum of three poems each. When you are finished, both of you hide your poems in secret places all around the house.

135. Love Letters
- Write your lover a romantic letter and send it to her office, or even back to your own home.

Thoughtful Ideas for Lovers

136. Love's Sweet Music
- Hire a harpist to serenade you.
- Write a romantic song for her, and then sing your heart out.

137. Announcing Your Love to the World
- Take out a classified ad affirming your love.
- Get a sky writer to write your names in the sky.
- Order a large pizza and spell out "I love you _____" with black olives, onions, or peppers.

138. Pictures of You

- Have a professional photographer shoot a romantic photo of the two of you.
- Have a portrait painted of the two of you together.
- Make your lover a surprise computer screen that opens up with a picture of the two of you.

139. Three Unexpected Gifts of Love

- Laminate a four-leaf clover onto a piece of paper. Write both of your names on the back and give it to him to keep in his wallet.
- Find paraphernalia (try eBay) of your lover's favorite performers, actors, or writers.
- Get a bicycle built for two. Spend your afternoons and weekends using love to maintain your momentum.

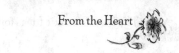

Romantic Treats for Anytime

140. Bringing Love to Work

- Show up at his office with his favorite meal in a picnic basket. To earn extra brownie points, bring enough for the whole office!
- Have a single rose and chocolate strawberries delivered to your lover's workplace.
- Bake a batch of fresh muffins and bring them to your lover's office.

141. Hungry for Your Love

Feeding one another is a wonderful, intimate way to show your love. Try feeding your lover M&Ms, cotton candy, or oysters. Take the time to experience the sensuality of the food in your mouth and your lover's fingers against your lips.

142. Sugar is Sweet and So Are You

- Leave a chocolate under the pillow for every day of the week.
- Leave a bag of Hershey's kisses on the dashboard.
- Leave a bag of Lifesavers in your lovers' pocket and write a note that says, "Our love has saved my life."

143. Flirting with Food

- Take turns sticking your clean toes into melted chocolate and painting each other's bodies. When the two of you are covered from head to toe, it's time to "clean up"!
- Write your lover's name on his hand in Pixie Stick candy and lick it off.
- Fill up two "His" and "Hers" bags with candy and naughty treats (e.g., edible underwear, edible and scented body lubricant, chocolate body paint).

144. Online Love

In today's fast-paced, high-tech society, the computer is often the only way to show our love during the day. Send your lover a romantic digital card or digital flower bouquet. If you are feeling particularly inspired, write a love letter to your partner via email.

Saying "I Love You" with Jewelry

145. Many lovers express their love for one another with jewelry. Try making your own accessories to add another dimension of love to your gift. A craftsy-looking piece made with true love and affection will always be worth a fortune in sentimental value.

146. That Has a Lovely Ring to It

- Give your lover a ring from a gumball machine, or a candy ring.
- Exchange the rings from expensive cigars.

147. Love the Skin She's In

Arrange to meet your lover for dinner at a romantic restaurant known for its atmosphere. Then, go to the makeup counter at your local department store and have the beautician give you a dramatic makeover. Who knows—your lover may not even recognize you! He'll appreciate you taking the time to really take care of yourself.

148. Sew in Love

- Embroider towels with both your initials.
- Knit a scarf for your lover.
- Get monogrammed pillowcases with both your initials on them.

Other-Worldly Love

149. Stars in Your Eyes

Perhaps the most loving gesture you could possibly make is to purchase a star for your lover. Many companies offer the opportunity to purchase and name a star for less than $100. While the ownership of the star is not recognized by NASA, you and your lover will spend the rest of your lives staring up at your special star with fondness. If you can't afford to buy one, simply choose one in the sky for your beloved!

150. The Mysticism of Love

- Read your lover's palm.
- See a psychic or hypnotist together.
- Drink tea and read your lover's tea leaves.
- Buy a bag of fortune cookies.
- Play with a Ouija board.

Love's Spellbinding Elixirs

151. Mix cranberry juice, pineapple juice, coconut milk, and orange juice, and serve with a strawberry or lime garnish. For more powerful magic, you can always add a little vodka!

152. Get a huge watermelon and a bottle of vodka or rum. Split the watermelon down the middle and pour the liquor all over it. Put the watermelon in the freezer for five to seven minutes. Then, indulge. Needless to say, this is a very sensual, heady experience!

153. Intoxicated by Love

- Dip raspberries or fruit slices into champagne, and then feed them to one another.
- Treat yourselves to a romantic, frivolous splurge and buy a bottle of 1967 Chateaux D'Yquem or a magnum of Crystal.

154. Your Most Treasured Possession

Love cannot flourish without trust. A wonderful exercise to prove your love and abiding trust for one another is to entrust your partner with your prized possession. Each of you choose a personal item that has special significance. Give them into each other's keeping, explaining what it means to you and why you want the other to have it.

155. The Sparkling Picture Board

What you need:

- Pictures, either taken with your camera or cut from a magazine, of things that represent what you would like to have in your romantic future
- A big piece of poster board
- Glue
- Colored glitter
- Construction paper
- Magic markers

Instructions

1. First, arrange the pictures on the poster board in collage fashion. As you glue them on the poster board, focus on the emotions behind enjoying true romantic fulfillment.

2. Write down inspirational romantic words on the colored paper with the magic

markers. As you write down the words, don't forget to feel their meaning.

3. When you have finished gluing on the words and pictures, lightly sprinkle the whole thing with colored glitter to add sparkle to your dreams.

4. Mount your completed board in a place where you can focus on it and enjoy it at any time.

Bet You Never Thought of This:

Unusual Romantic Activities for the Adventurous

Love Is an Adventure

156. Water Music

- For a beautiful summertime experience, share the wonder and intimacy of diving or snorkeling in the deep blue sea.
- Summer is a great time to go cascading downriver while white-water rafting. Feel the cool water splash over you, as you and your lover scream with sheer delight.
- Romance runs high when the surf is up! Even if you and your lover are not exactly Malibu Barbie and Ken, you can still grab a surfboard and make a valiant attempt to conquer the tide.

157. Love and Adrenaline

- If you and your lover are really into wild rides and junk food, find the closest amusement park and have yourselves a rip-roaring, exhilarating time together.

- Rent a glider plane.
- Zip across a wide, open field in a snow-mobile. Grab on to your honey as you zoom off into the white plateau.

158. Milk Your Love for All It's Worth

As bizarre as it sounds, milking a cow together will create an atmosphere of wonder and surprise that will exhilarate you both. The fact that the two of you are willing to do something like this shows great versatility, adaptability, and a willingness to stretch your boundaries for one another —the ultimate gift of love. This back-to-basics romantic experience is sure to moo-ve your relationship to a deeper level.

159. Hypnotized by Love

Hypnotize your lover. Ask him to lie down on a couch and get comfortable. Then, tell him to count backwards from one hundred. When he gets to the number one, he should be totally relaxed. Give him romantic suggestions, like, "On the count of three, you find me absolutely irresistible and can't stop kissing me." Count to three, snap your fingers, and see what happens!

160. Witness the Miracle of Birth

There is nothing more romantic than witnessing the miracle of birth together. You and your lover can go to any farm or stable in your area to watching this profound process taking place. Doing something like this helps take the focus off of the everyday grind of your relationship, and helps spread the joy around.

161. Flying High on Love

- For the romantic thrill of a lifetime, sail over land and sea in a hot-air balloon. Spend the day or just go for an hour or two. The two of you can take turns screaming "I love you" at the top of your lungs for all the world to hear!
- Summer is a great time to hop on a Harley and head cross-country. You may find yourselves inscribing your names on each other's forearms (or other body parts)!

162. Love's Cabaret

For a change of pace in your normal entertainment, find yourselves a smoky cabaret featuring music from the '40s and '50s. As you have a couple of drinks and listen to the singer belt out the blues, the seedy environment will seduce you.

163. Defend Your Lover

This spring, you and your lover might enjoy doing something to build your mental and physical strength: a beginner martial arts class. When you and your lover realize how strong and powerful you both are, it will add a whole other dimension to the relationship.

164. Take Me to the North Pole

If you and your lover are up for the ultimate in adventure travel, take a trip to the North Pole. Spend a week ice fishing and rubbing noses with the local Eskimos in an igloo. Take a walk around Glacier Bay National Park in Alaska, where you can see ice-blue icebergs, watch the glaciers advance, and take a sweet day cruise through spectacular scenery.

165. When Lovers Misbehave...

- Visit a sex shop. Giggle at the merchandise.
- Make love outside your house.
- "Misbehave" while waiting for a table in a restaurant.

Love in Its Natural Form

166. The nude beach is a simple, yet adventurous way to add a bit of extra fun to sun-filled days. You and your lover will enjoy the uninhibited sense of freedom as you frolic shamelessly in the waves and bury more than just your toes in the sand.

167. For those of you who enjoy nude beaches, try visiting a real nudist colony for more summertime fun. Run uninhibited with your lover beneath the warm sunlight.

Gone with the Wind

168. Another great romantic sport is wind surfing. Learning is half the fun, especially if you have a lover helping you to get up and grab hold of the sail. Wind surfing is very romantic because the two of you will find yourselves tangled together again and again.

169. Is it a bird? Is it a plane? No, it's the super-lovers parasailing high above the clear, blue bay. Imagine, you and your lover side by side, floating through the air on a parasailer. What a romantic feeling of love and freedom as you and your lover kiss the clouds goodbye.

170. Announce Your Love to the World

- Get matching tattoos.
- Get T-shirts with "I ❤ ____" and fill in each other's names.
- Rent a billboard and declare your love.

Love in the Stars:

Astrology Insights for Lovers

Gifts from the Stars: Astrology-Inspired Ideas

171. Top Ten Romantic Gifts for a Pisces

1. Music by Enya.
2. Any book by the Dalai Lama.
3. *Soul Love* by Sanaya Roman.
4. A weekend at a yoga retreat or ashram.
5. Yoga lessons.
6. Any book on meditation.
7. A trip to the Vatican or to Jerusalem.
8. A psychic or aura reading.
9. A book or CD by Dr. Wayne Dyer.
10. A weekend at Deepak Chopra's Ayurvedic spa in La Jolla, California, or any book by Deepak Chopra.

172. Top Ten Romantic Gifts for an Aries

1. A head/scalp massage.
2. An appointment with the most expensive hairdresser or barber in town.
3. A personalized diary with pictures of him/her in it.
4. An antique mirror.
5. *The Art of War* by Lao Tzu
6. *The Art of the Deal* by Donald Trump, or anything by Donald Trump, including a weekend get-away to Mar-A-Lago, his posh club in Palm Beach, Florida.
7. A handmade parchment scroll that lists, "The Ten Things I Love about You."
8. A gorgeous fur hat or any kind of expensive hat.
9. A diamond tiara for a woman, a smoking jacket for a man.
10. Anything monogrammed or personalized with your lover's name on it.

173. Top Ten Romantic Gifts for a Taurus

1. A gourmet meal at the hottest restaurant in town.
2. A bag of chocolate money or candy dollar bills.
3. A new duvet.
4. A La-Z-Boy recliner.
5. Breakfast, lunch, and dinner in bed.
6. Edible underwear and flavored body gels.
7. A weekend away at an inn famous for its large country breakfasts.
8. A lottery ticket.
9. Any book or video that tells you how to use food with sex.
10. French or Italian cooking lessons.

174. Top Ten Romantic Gifts for a Gemini

1. Fur earmuffs.
2. A new computer game.
3. A VIP pass to the hottest nightclub in town.
4. A getaway where you do something different every day.
5. A new outfit or pair of shoes that reflect the latest fashion.
6. A membership to the gym.
7. A different tie or scarf for every day of the week.
8. A trip to a new city.
9. A diamond stud earring.
10. A temporary tattoo kit.

175. Top Ten Romantic Gifts for a Cancer

1. A family album.
2. A certificate to a company website that traces his/her family tree.
3. A magazine or book that show how to redecorate or add on to your home.
4. A trip to see a relative who lives far away.
5. A handmade parchment scroll that lists, "100 Reasons Why I Love You."
6. A book of children's names.
7. A trip to the country of his/her ethnic heritage.
8. Take her shopping for a new home.
9. A mood ring.
10. An artist's easel or drawing board.

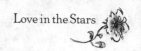

176. Top Ten Romantic Gifts for a Leo

1. A trip to Miami or any sunny climate.
2. A tanning bed.
3. An expensive self-tanning set.
4. A book of European royalty and castles.
5. Biographies of the world's most famous leaders.
6. Biographies of the world's most famous celebrities.
7. A handmade parchment scroll that lists, "Why I Think You Could Rule the World."
8. Have an artist paint a portrait of your lover in a regal outfit.
9. A big gold chain.
10. Anything that says "You Are the King of My Heart" on it.

177. Top Ten Romantic Gifts for a Virgo

1. A how-to book on anything.
2. Send a cleaning crew or a maid to clean your lovers' house from top to bottom.
3. The DVD *Analyze This* with Billy Crystal and Robert DeNiro.
4. Hire a company to organize the closet.
5. Have all his/her shoes polished.
6. Have all his/her suits cleaned and pressed.
7. A custom-made suit or gown.
8. If you live together, arrange all your stuff the way they do theirs.
9. An exotic-wine, foreign-language, or financial-investing course.
10. A handmade parchment scroll that lists, "Ten Reasons Why I Think You're Perfect."

178. Top Ten Romantic Gifts for a Libra

1. A trip to a smorgasbord buffet.
2. A subscription to the *National Enquirer*, the *Globe*, and *Star*.
3. Tickets to a Tony Robbins seminar.
4. *The Power of Positive Thinking* by Dale Carnegie.
5. A weekend getaway to a place you know he loves, but would never admit it.
6. A big piece of jewelry.
7. A trip to the United Nations.
8. Tickets to a big celebrity benefit.
9. A whole day of pampering at a day spa.
10. A fun, flashy sports car.

179. Top Ten Romantic Gifts for a Scorpio

1. *The Kama Sutra*.
2. A subscription to *Oui* magazine.
3. A new collection of adult tapes.
4. Frank Sinatra's *Greatest Hits* (all volumes).
5. *The Art of Seduction* by Robert Greene.
6. *Tapping Into Your Own Psychic Ability* by Edgar Cayce.
7. *Forever* by Judy Blume.
8. A trip to Italy.
9. A trip to Hugh Hefner's Playboy Mansion.
10. A gift from the Frederick's of Hollywood catalog.

180. Top Ten Romantic Gifts for a Sagittarius

1. Tickets to an ice-hockey match.
2. Tickets to the Winter Olympics or any other major winter event.
3. A trip to Switzerland or anywhere that offers serious skiing.
4. A trip to the Andes.
5. Flying lessons.
6. A pass to jump out of an airplane the following spring.
7. An African safari.
8. A trip through the rainforest.
9. A cruise through Alaska.
10. The most up-to-date, cutting edge, and expensive electronic gadget on the market.

181. Top Ten Romantic Gifts for a Capricorn

1. A life-insurance policy.
2. Exercise equipment with a thirty-day guarantee.
3. Arrange for them to go to a taping of *Antiques Road Show*.
4. Take them to the snootiest antique auction in your area.
5. Special lights that prevent seasonal affective disorder.
6. United States Treasury Bills.
7. Paint their bedroom bright yellow.
8. A winter's supply of St. John's Wort.
9. A trip to the area where their favorite type of antiques come from.
10. A guide to celebrity homes.

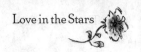

Love in the Stars

182. Top Ten Romantic Gifts for an Aquarius

1. Tickets to a Murder Mystery party.
2. A big birthday party.
3. A tie-dyed sweatshirt.
4. The soundtrack from *La Cage Aux Folles* featuring the song "I Am What I Am," or Sinatra's "I Did It My Way."
5. A signed poster of James Dean or any other famous rebel (with or without a cause).
6. *Romantic Intuition* by Laura Bailey.
7. A membership to a gym with an indoor pool.
8. Ask what their wackiest fantasy is, then make it happen.
9. One really expensive item.
10. A sexy ankle bracelet.

97

Astrological Couplings

183. **Aries/Aries:** These two fiery souls may butt heads sometimes, but they also have a very deep understanding of each other. The secret of success for two Aries mates is to love each other with the passion and intensity that you love yourselves. If you feel the need to fight, remember that you are on the same romantic team. When the two of you can learn to give just a little bit, you will have an exciting romantic relationship.

184. **Aries/Taurus**: An Aries can brighten a Taurus's life by helping him or her stretch their imagination and boundaries of intimacy. If you are both willing to be open to one another's suggestions and not force your will all the time, these two signs will have a fine romance.

185. **Aries/Gemini**: This relationship has the potential for a lot of fun. When teamed up in a romance, both these signs exhibit their child-like, playful qualities. You two will have a great time dreaming up a grand plan to take over the world. The key romantic word here is consideration.

186. Aries/Cancer: While the Aries individual tends to forge through life with courage and ambition, Cancer is a more cautious sign. The Aries lover must take into consideration that their Cancer partner might not always be ready to go full speed ahead. On the other hand, the Cancer in the relationship should be careful about slowing the Aries down or holding him/her back. The secret to this romance is understanding and balance. Sometimes it's best to ride with the wind, and other times it's great to stop and smell the flowers!

187. Aries/Leo: You two can have a wonderful romance if you are willing to avoid competing and enjoy basking in each other's glory. Both Aries and Leo love to be at the top of the heap. You will make a wonderful couple if you realize that the red carpet is long enough for both

of you. This is the key to your happy and glamorous future!

188. **Aries/Virgo:** In this love combo, you have a pairing of real opposites. The Aries makes decisions based on strong urges and emotions, while the Virgo is practical and calculating. This can be a good match if the Virgo can remember not to be too critical of the Aries' heated personality, and the Aries sometimes allow themselves to be reined in when they go off on a fiery tangent. With plenty of love and encouragement, you two can support each other through anything.

189. **Aries/Libra:** The great thing about Libra and Aries people is that these two can really learn to complement each other. When the Aries gets passionately irate about something, the Libra reacts with a calmer countenance. The Libra's life is enriched by

the Aries' passion and energy. At the end of the day, the Ram will lovingly and gratefully retreat into Libra's embrace.

190. **Aries/Scorpio:** Scorpio is the sign that can keep the rambunctious Ram on its toes! Their styles are very different—while the Ram will go gallivanting around issuing challenges, the Scorpion will sit silently until ready to strike. The bottom line in this relationship is that the Ram must be able to trust the Scorpion. If both signs acknowledge, respect, and honor each other's power, they will have a very strong romance.

191. **Aries/Sagittarius:** This is an enthusiastic, high-powered, sometimes over-the-top relationship. The Ram and the Archer could save the whales or accomplish anything else they take

on, since they both excel at fighting for a cause. Make sure to spend some intimate time together to cement your relationship, and you'll be ready to take on the world!

192. **Aries/Capricorn:** It is hard for Capricorn not to be envious of Aries' enthusiasm, and for Aries to be patient with Capricorn's steady ways. Capricorn, take pride in the stability you can provide in the relationship, but be willing to lighten up. Aries, you can help Capricorn look for laughter, and you two will find a love that works.

193. **Aries/Aquarius:** This has the makings of a good relationship because both signs enjoy a devil-may-care attitude toward life. They are always ready for a party and even more ready to plan for a bright tomorrow. Spontaneity and excitement keep these

two signs in a revved-up, red-hot romance. Enjoy each other, and don't forget to help one another stay grounded.

194. **Aries/Pisces:** At first glance, you would think that the hot-headed Aries would be tempted to push around the people-pleasing Pisces. But consider that Pisces is a water sign, and water can put out fire in one good swoosh! The Aries lover should be careful not to take advantage of the Pisces's good nature. If the Aries can enjoy the Pisces's gentleness and not push too hard, water and fire will exist in harmony!

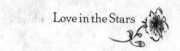

195. Taurus/Taurus: What a sublime, comfy, cozy time these two bulls can have together relaxing in their pen! This combination has the makings of a sensuous, gourmet romance filled with the best of everything. The beauty of it is that most of your arguments can be resolved with a vintage bottle of wine, a fine meal, and a hot-oil massage.

196. Taurus/Gemini: While Bulls might not take kindly to Gemini's flighty, flirtatious ways, they will be enticed by the Twins' quick mental adaptability and fun nature. The Bull can act as a real stabilizing force to balance the Gemini's tendency to be all over the place. If the bull can learn not to be threatened by the Gemini's flashing eyes and devilish smile, and the Twins can put up with the Bull's possessiveness, they will enjoy an exhilarating romance.

197. Taurus/Cancer: Home sweet home! Because the Crab and Bull both love home and family, this combination is a natural winner. They will share a similar value system that will make the romance feel safe, as well as passionate. A good snuggle under the covers and comforting hugs will soothe both savage beasts.

198. Taurus/Leo: Glory, glory, Hallelujah! What do you do with two animals that need to be loved and adored twenty-four hours a day? Simple: you make your romance a mutual admiration society. Honor each other's need to be respected and admired. These two robust signs will share a lush palace and get along just fine if they let each other be king for a day.

199. Taurus/Virgo: Practically speaking, these two down-to-earth souls are a good romantic match. They both have a straightforward approach to life and they are not going to let anyone take advantage of them. If the Virgo can loosen up a bit and the Taurus can learn not to take everything to heart, these two earth signs will enjoy a satisfying romance.

200. Taurus/Libra: Since Libras are so good at remaining diplomatic, they have a good chance of shrugging it off if Taurus acts like a bull in a china shop. The Bull might feel the need to start making decisions to compensate for Libra's indecisiveness. This can work out fine as long as Libra agrees with what Taurus has in mind. A romance can flourish here when Libra learns to stay on top of a bucking steer and go with the flow.

201. Taurus/Scorpio: On a physical level, this relationship has the potential to be hot, hot, hot! However, once these two get out of the bedroom, issues of control and honesty could arise. While the Scorpio tends to be demanding, the Bull is not one to be told what to do. Taurus is straightforward and expects the same of their partner, which may not always be easy for the subtle Scorpio. If these signs can appreciate their sensuous relationship and cut each other some slack in other areas, the opportunities for a sizzling romance are endless.

202. Taurus/Sagittarius: The challenge here is one that is basic to the underlying natures of these two signs. While the Taurus wants to be comfortable in a luxurious home, the Sagittarius wants to be off traveling and discovering the world. If you can compromise, you can

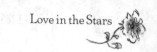

have the best of both worlds. Sagittarius, agree to stay home for a while and plan your next adventure, and Taurus, agree to accompany the Sagittarius on an exquisite gourmet vacation! Fly the Taurus first class and make sure the hotel has a good restaurant, and the Sag will see that his/her homebody lover is far from boring.

203. **Taurus/Capricorn**: This is one of the steady, sturdy, meat and potatoes relationships in the Zodiac. Both signs are dependable and reliable—you could set a stopwatch by these people's habits. Since stability is their romantic secret, they are free to pursue other avenues (such as career) to great success. Their passion may not seem fiery in nature, but it is marked by a smoldering intensity that will endure.

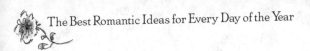

204. **Taurus/Aquarius:** This is a challenging relationship because, while the air sign of Aquarius tends to revel in flights of fancy and exploration, the Taurus's feet remain planted firmly on the ground. Aquarius are lovable geniuses with potential to drive a Taurus crazy, while Aquarians may feel stifled by the Taurus's need to be steady and unchanging. What an opportunity to learn from each other! If you both keep your minds open, Taurus can be lifted to new heights, and Aquarius can revel in sensuous comfort they might otherwise never experience.

205. **Taurus/Pisces:** While the Pisces is lost in a spiritual quest, the Taurus is going over their credit card bills. Strangely enough, this mix of heaven and earth can result in a really satisfying romance that works for both. The Pisces will allow the Taurus to teach him/her how to function in

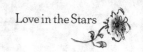

the real world, while the Taurus is comforted by the Fish's gentle spirit. Conflicts could arise when the Pisces wants to take the Bull up to a mountain to meditate. If the Fish can remember and respect the fact that Bulls like their creature comforts, these two will have no problem.

206. **Gemini/Gemini:** This is a fast-moving, exciting whirl of a good time. These two people are so busy doing, coming, going, seeing, and being that they don't have much time to slow down and analyze their relationship—and they don't have to. They understand each other's need for freedom and space. Lest they whirl past each other too often without stopping, the double twin combo does need to take time out for each other on occasion, just to hold hands and reconnect.

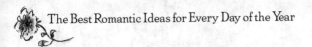

207. Gemini/Cancer: While the basic natures of the Crab and the Twins are very different, they can actually balance each other out very successfully. Recognize and appreciate your differences. While the Gemini needs to be running around, buzzing full speed ahead, the Cancer would rather be focusing on home and family. If the Gemini allows himself/herself to be calmed and comforted by the Cancer and the Cancer relaxes his/her need to have things under control, these two can ride off into the sunset happily.

208. Gemini/Leo: The Twins and the Lion both share the need to show the world that they are at the top of their game. They avoid power struggles with each other because their approaches are so different. The Leo has an innate, regal, lazy sense of

entitlement. The Twins spends their whole life rushing around on the go. These two will always make sure that they enjoy the best of everything in life and love.

209. **Gemini/Virgo:** This one almost mirrors a parent-child relationship because the Gemini is a kid at heart, and the Virgo is a mature, serious sign. The Virgo, who always strives for perfection, may have trouble with the Gemini's constant flitting about. Virgo, don't be too critical or expect the Twins to settle down and grow up, something they are not too willing to do. Treat each other with care and respect, and you'll find your love will grow.

210. **Gemini/Libra:** This relationship seems to be pretty happy-go-lucky. The ever-changing Gemini and the easygoing Libra usually appear to be

all sunshine and roses. Of course, Libra, who is so used to being able to persuade, may be surprised when Gemini doesn't do what he/she wants. And Gemini may find it all too easy to drive Libra crazy with his/her elusiveness. Keep your expectations of each other realistic, and don't succumb to the temptation to seek the upper hand, and you two can enjoy a delightful romance.

211. **Gemini/Scorpio**: The Twins and the Scorpion have potential for a very passionate romance, although there are a few potential pitfalls stemming from their differences. While the Gemini likes to be the outgoing, vivacious life of the party, the sexy-but-silent Scorpio feels more powerful remaining reserved. A little work on building trust and appreciation will ensure a great romance for the Twins and Scorpion.

212. **Gemini/Sagittarius:** As a team, these two high-energy, motivated people can inspire each other to do great things. Both signs have very few limitations. What they lack as a couple is grounding. Since there is no calming, stabilizing force here, they can blow each other away. The Twins and the Archer should be cautious about getting in each other's way. The secret is to stay committed to living in reality while shooting for the stars.

213. **Gemini/Capricorn:** Since Capricorns love anything having to do with fame, they see the Twins as a constant source of entertainment. This brings great happiness to a relationship. Gemini is a whimsical air sign and Capricorn is planted firmly on earth. Look past your surface differences for ways to deepen your love and intimacy. You can have a lot of fun together,

and enjoy being a different, but lovely, couple!

214. **Gemini/Aquarius**: Geminis are constantly in motion and have a tendency to dance their way around the truth. While Aquarians love the unconventional and have a high tolerance for change, they are exacting people and demand tangible results. However, these two lovers can have a fine romance if the Gemini is willing to make an effort to be more straightforward and the Aquarius is willing to relax his/her almost impossibly high standards.

215. **Gemini/Pisces**: While the Gemini is a high-action mover and shaker, the Pisces tends to be more of a quiet soul. This can work both for and against these two lovers. If the Pisces is willing to join the Gemini lover and race with the wind, and the

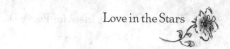

Gemini is ready to take the Pisces under his or her wing, a diversified romance can thrive.

216. **Cancer/Cancer**: If these two lovers can come out of their corners, trust each other, and open up with their true feelings, they will find the comfort of a kindred spirit. It takes one Crab to fully understand the emotional needs of another Cancer soul. If the Crabs are in a sulky mood, they can look to each other for sympathy. This match can develop into a very nurturing, comforting romance.

217. **Cancer/Leo**: These two can find peace and love if Leo is willing to let the Crab sulk without taking it personally. Lion, remember that the moodiness of the gentle Crab doesn't necessarily have to do with you. Crab, come out of hiding and recognize the

Lion's need for admiration and attention. Love and support one another, and it's possible for these two widely different signs to thrive in a relationship.

218. **Cancer/Virgo**: The great thing these lovers have going for them is that the relationship starts from a standpoint of peace and serenity. The perfectionist Virgo is immediately soothed and calmed by the gentle Crab, and isn't bothered by his/her occasional moodiness. The Crab is reassured by the confident Virgo. So, if the Virgo can keep the need for perfection in check and the Crab can remain calm and grounded, these two lovers will enjoy smooth sailing.

219. **Cancer/Libra**: The key to this relationship is a sense of humor. Even though a Libra is basically good-

natured and tolerant, a Crab's constant need for love and compassion may be a little hard to handle. Focus on keeping a lot of fun in your lives, and Cancer and Libra can laugh their way into eternity.

220. **Cancer/Scorpio:** This is a romance sent from heaven! Although there can be occasional power struggles, this is a fairly graceful love match. Both signs are great at being supportive of each other, because they are naturally supportive in general. The Cancer also really appreciates the Scorpion's deep sensuality, which makes the Crab feel loved and wanted—very important to his/her sense of security. All you two have to do is be thankful for the ease of the relationship, and don't create any unnecessary complications.

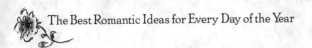

221. Cancer/Sagittarius: If a Sagittarius really loves his/her Cancer mate, he/she will go the extra mile to make sure the Crab is handled with tender loving care. In this relationship, the Sagittarius lover may not realize how deeply his/her sharp arrows can hurt the gentle soul of the Crab. The happy, upbeat Sagittarius has to learn tact and sensitivity, and the Cancer partner should recognize that being with Sagittarius can bring much joy into his/her life.

222. Cancer/Capricorn: These two opposites have exactly what the other wants and needs to feel loved and cherished. This romantic relationship works best when the two lovers learn to capitalize on each other's strengths, because they are so different. While the Cancer has a softer, kinder approach to life, the Capricorn tends to be tougher,

but stable and dependable. The Crab likes the fact he/she can lean on and look up to the Capricorn. The Capricorn feels he/she can relax in the Crab's presence. This makes for a very balanced and energetic romance.

223. **Cancer/Aquarius**: This relationship is a lot more compatible than it appears on the surface. That is because both of these signs are comfortable with change and unpredictability. Since Aquarius loves the unconventional and outra-geous, he/she isn't at all bothered by the Cancer's changing countenance. The Aquarius doesn't think that the Cancer is too sensitive; rather, he/she likes the fact that the Cancer isn't afraid to show emotions. At first, the Cancer may be a bit in awe of the brilliant Aquarius. However, as the romance progresses, the Crab will learn to delight in his/her water-bearing lover.

224. **Cancer/Pisces:** This is a very mellow romance. Because both signs are soft, sweet-natured, and amenable, there is not a lot of conflict here. Of course, both Cancer and Pisces can be manipulative in their own ways, but there is not a lot of time and energy in this relationship given to that. The Crab and the Fish just seem to float along through life, providing support, understanding, and reassurance. This is a romance that thrives on healing their feelings.

225. **Leo/Leo:** If these two big cats can play nice and learn not to scratch each other's eyes out, then an earthshaking romance will be theirs. Both people in this powerful relationship must take turns being the leader. That is not so simple for two proud lovers who both want to reign over their kingdom. Still, with a lot of love and

patience, these two monster kitties can be tamed in the name of romance.

226. Leo/Virgo: This is a very majestic, luminous relationship, because the Virgo is comfortable letting the Leo be the king of the jungle. As a matter of fact, the Virgo enjoys being behind the scenes, making sure that everything is running to perfection backstage. Both partners will need to keep their critical natures in check at times. Romance hits a high note here when the Leo gets a standing ovation and acknowledges that he/she couldn't have gotten there without his/her Virgo.

227. Leo/Libra: This romance requires the Leo to really stretch and be open to something besides being the ruling party. Although it is not really in a Libra's nature to start a fight, it is important to weigh both sides of an issue. If the Lion can be patient and the Libra can learn to make decisions a little more quickly, then these two can enjoy a thought-provoking romance.

228. Leo/Scorpio: In this relationship, the Lion has finally met his match. As much as Leo would love to dominate this lover, the Scorpion will stand for no such thing. There is more mutual respect here than power struggle, because Scorpio knows the power of his/her sting. The Scorpio has no problem putting a collar around the big cat's neck and keeping him/her on a tight leash. Even though the lion never loses his/her sense of regal pride, Leo automatically becomes much more of a "benevolent despot" when romancing a spicy Scorpion.

229. Leo/Sagittarius: There is a good dose of healthy competition going on here, day in and day out. In fact, the Lion and the Archer can create the Olympiad of romantic relationships. Just be sure to appreciate the vitality in the relationship and give up the battle long enough to kiss each other good night.

230. Leo/Capricorn: Since Capricorn loves fame, wealth, and notoriety, being with the King of the Jungle is quite a treat. The Lion will find that the stubborn Goat is not easy to dominate. However, Capricorn so admires Leo's aura of glamour, he/she is usually willing to be accommodating. That works for the Leo, and everybody's romantic dreams are fulfilled.

231. Leo/Aquarius: Leo is mystified and fascinated by Aquarius's boldness. This creates a very interesting relationship. There is something very seductive to the Lion about Aquarian audacity and bucking of convention. The Leo has the confidence to let the Aquarius push forth bravely into the unknown without looking back. The Aquarius can respect and admire Leo's strength and confidence. Together, the Leo and Aquarius can break through boundaries and thrive in a love without limitations.

232. Leo/Pisces: For the Pisces that doesn't mind being dominated, this is a perfect love match. In a subtle way, it is almost easier for the Pisces to live under the rule of the Lion because it relieves him/her of the very tough decision making he/she would just as soon ignore. It can be very liberating

for a Pisces to let the Lion rule the roost, and the Lion is very comfortable in this role. The Pisces can follow his/her spiritual pursuits knowing that worldly concerns are being taken care of by very competent big paws.

233. **Virgo/Virgo:** When two Virgos engage in a romance, they need to get clear what's important and what's not right away. Two perfectionists struggling with different definitions of what perfection really is can drive each other crazy. The good news is that two Virgos with a similar value system and worldview will be able to strive together in one positive direction. They can kill themselves joyfully getting it right all the time, unhampered by the restrictions a less fastidious partner might impose.

234. Virgo/Libra: In this romance, the Virgo has to be extra careful not to kill the Libra's exuberance. Virgo, be aware that the Libra may not want to hear your accurate but thorny observations. Let him/her be, and Libra can go along making life beautiful. Virgo must learn to be grateful for such a colorful and pleasing lover. The Libra should go on his/her merry way, realizing that he can't please everybody all the time.

235. Virgo/Scorpio: This relationship can be a real challenge for the Virgo because the hot, passionate Scorpion defies logic. There is nothing calculated about this romance at all, and that can really get the Virgo flustered. What a marvelous thing! Being involved with a Scorpio forces the Virgo to live on the edge and let go. This is a real growth situation and a heck of a

lot of fun for the Scorpion, who loves to seduce the practical Virgin.

236. Virgo/Sagittarius: This romance keeps moving forward because the Sagittarius has the great ability to keep the Virgo interested and stimulated. To the perfection-loving Virgo, the fact that the Sagittarius is constantly on the move and exploring the world is absolutely fabulous. The Virgo knows that a romance with a Sagittarius will broaden his/her horizons and keep him/her learning new things. The Virgo feels most useful when he/she can "perfect" all the exciting things that the Sagittarius brings to the relationship.

237. **Virgo/Capricorn**: When a Virgo and a Capricorn team up, you have a couple dedicated to holding up the moral and social fiber of our nation. They will take great joy in supporting their community, forwarding important causes, and pursuing truth and justice. They will have much cause to be proud of one another, and there will be no lack of energy in their romance. This passionate, upstanding duo makes an outstanding pair!

238. **Virgo/Aquarius**: This relationship is fascinating because the Virgo lives to have everything in life just so, and the Aquarius lives to cause total chaos. This romance can stretch the boundaries of both. Virgo and Aquarius will thrive together when they focus on what they can learn from each other, and be proud and tolerant of their differences.

239. **Virgo/Pisces**: This relationship runs best when the Fish is content and willing to let their lover steer the ship. The Virgo loves to take charge, and as long as the Pisces doesn't rebel, all is romantically well here. Pisces should be careful not to hide feelings of displeasure from the Virgo. If Pisces is not straightforward, the Virgo doesn't know how to handle it. Keep the channels of communication open and romance will grow freely.

240. **Libra/Libra**: This bright, happy, open, communicative relationship is terrific, as long as these two highly intelligent "sparklers" are comfortable with all that sunshine. Sometimes, a rainy day can be great for spending the day in bed and cuddling. The Libra lovers must learn to enjoy the downtime along with the rainbows and firecrackers. If

two Libras can accomplish this, then
no matter what the weather, their
romance will be coming up roses.

241. **Libra/Scorpio**: In this romance, the
seductive but settled Scorpion has a
positive effect on the energetic but
sometimes scattered Libra. Libra
knows that he/she is in a powerful
presence when in a romance with the
Scorpio. Although the Libra may
never fully understand the Scorpion's
secrecy and confidence, he/she can
respect and even admire the unique
ways a Scorpion partner. In return,
the Scorpion is thoroughly delighted
by his/her lighthearted lover. This is
romance filled with respect and good
old-fashioned giddiness.

242. **Libra/Sagittarius:** Although this is a fun-filled, enthusiastic, very successful relationship most of the time, it is not without some bumps along the road. The Sagittarius can be a little too direct and stick an arrow through Libra's delicate heart. Libra is a sensitive soul who sometimes hides behind a shining smile. The Sagittarius must make it a point not to take this for granted. With a little tact and honesty, these two lovers can have a wonderful time on their mutual quest to live life to the fullest.

243. **Libra/Capricorn:** A Libra is born to fly and won't be easy to hold down. At the same time, a Libra can love and appreciate the constant stability that a Capricorn brings to a romance. Recognize and acknowledge that these signs are very different souls right from the start. If the

Capricorn can let himself have a good laugh and the Libra can use that famous diplomacy when necessary, an enjoyable romance will be theirs.

244. **Libra/Aquarius**: Both parties in a Libra/Aquarius relationship are used to being a little unconventional. The Aquarian gets a kick out of being crazy in the far-out, rebellious sense of the word. To the Libra, crazy means shaving-cream fights on Halloween and sack races with third-graders. The secret for these two is to avoid competing for the spotlight and not try to outdo each other. If Libra and Aquarius want to stay romantically entwined, then they have to realize that there is enough craziness to go around in this world.

245. **Libra/Pisces**: This is a very balanced romance because both signs really love

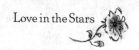

each other's softer side. The sensitive Pisces is refreshed by the Libra's bubbly persona and appreciates the Libra's diplomacy. The Libra feels loved and comfortable because he/she knows that he/she isn't going to be torn apart emotionally. In this warm, safe romance, both lovers are free to live, breathe, and fantasize to each other's delight.

246. **Scorpio/Scorpio:** The double Scorpion relationship is a deeply passionate romance with an intriguing air of mystery. The pitfall for two Scorpions is competitiveness—who can keep the most secrets, who can be the more sexually adventurous, and who is still more attractive to people outside the relationship. Scorpions feel best when they have the upper hand, so loving someone of their own sign can be tricky. However,

when these two lovers allow themselves to get in sync, it is a sensuous celebration worth everything they put into it.

247. **Scorpio/Sagittarius**: As with any challenging match, the potential rewards here are great. Scorpio may wish that Sagittarius would slow down long enough for a nice, hot bath and a massage. While Sagittarius is attracted to Scorpio's air of mystery, he/she's not really comfortable with having to guess at a lover's true feelings. When Scorpio is willing to open up and Sagittarius is willing to curb some of his/her sharpness, then their romance can be deeply satisfying to both.

248. Scorpio/Capricorn: This romance is based on both lovers' desires for respect, trust, and confidence. While both signs tend to feel superior, in this relationship their confidence works in their favor because it allows both of them to feel relaxed and at ease with each other. Not only that, the Capricorn is thrilled by the sexy Scorpion's aura of power and sensuousness. And while Scorpio relates well to Capricorn's settled approach to life, he/she also enjoys the effect he/she can have on a normally reserved Capricorn.

249. Scorpio/Aquarius: This is a highly charged romance. The Aquarius' outrageousness doesn't always sit well with the silent Scorpion. The Aquarius doesn't really understand his/her lover's deep reserve. As with any pairing of opposites, the key is to respect each other's differences.

Aquarius can win Scorpio's trust by not making light of the secrets that Scorpio wishes to protect. Scorpio can accept the high-flying Aquarius and be willing to crack his/her protective shell enough to let his/her lover in.

250. **Scorpio/Pisces:** This is a heaven-sent relationship with a deeply spiritual connection. For reasons unknown to the outside world, these two lovers are very much in tune with each other's desires and needs. Somehow, they know instinctively how to take care of one another. This doesn't usually involve much talking or discussion. The romantic communication is done on another level. To watch these two is to observe two lovers moving in perfect harmony with each other.

251. **Sagittarius/Sagittarius**: A little
kindness and consideration will go a
long way in making this relationship
work. You would think that because
these two lovers are so heavily influ-
enced by Jupiter, their relationship
would be filled with endless positive
expansion. Unfortunately, the
abundance of wanderlust and frank-
ness that characterizes this sign can
wreak havoc on the egos of two
Sagittarius lovers in a romantic pair.
Remember what you love about each
other, and enjoy a vigorous
romance.

252. **Sagittarius/Capricorn**: Oddly
enough, the settled, stable Capricorn
is delighted by the flighty Sagittarius.
As a matter of fact, Capricorns find
a Sagittarius's endless quest for the
world's jewels a real plus, attracted as
he/she is to fame and fortune.
Capricorn is invigorated by the

Archer's enthusiasm and energy. Because the Capricorn is so sharp and well-versed, the Sagittarius doesn't seem to mind a sometimes staid demeanor. Strangely, the Capricorn's bouts of selfishness can be very appealing to the Sagittarius simply because he/she understands it so well. Therefore, these strange bedfellows can have a romance that is as solid as it is spicy.

253. **Sagittarius/Aquarius**: These two freedom-loving signs know no boundaries. A romance between a Sagittarius and an Aquarius is likely to be a spectacular affair marked by brilliance, humor, and mind-blowing accomplishment—if they don't get arrested. When all is said and done, the Sagittarius and Aquarius will share a legendary love and a life without limitations.

254. Sagittarius/Pisces: In this romance, you have one fast-talking, energetic, hard-nosed optimist and one soft-spoken, watery dreamer. Sometimes the strangest combinations work! The good news for the Sagittarius is that they don't have to worry about the Fish judging them or questioning their haphazard travels. The Pisces is not inclined to quell the Sagittarius's sense of adventure because it is not a sign that has to stay in one place to feel secure. The Pisces will encourage the Sagittarius to stop and think before they speak, which is not a bad thing for a Sagittarius to learn. With a lot of love and mutual respect, this romance can go swimmingly.

255. Capricorn/Capricorn: Like the antiques that the Capricorn loves to collect, this romance gets better with time. When these two lovers are just starting out in life, it is their natural inclination to do things on the straight and narrow. As they mature, however, their need to live by the book loosens up quite a bit. In their later years, the more frivolous, fun-loving side of the Capricorn takes over. In fact, the sooner two Capricorns decide that life is too short for restrictions, the party and the romance will really take off.

256. Capricorn/Aquarius: It's hard to generalize about this relationship. The success of this romance is going to depend upon the tolerance and patience of the individuals. It is instinctive to the Aquarius to shake things up. However, the Capricorn loves everything to be in order and

under control. If both lovers are absolutely committed to each other and willing to do things that don't necessarily come naturally, their romance will thrive despite any astrological differences.

257. **Capricorn/Pisces:** This is a match of opposites that can harmonize beautifully. The Pisces loves the sense of stability and security that the Capricorn provides and in turn, the Capricorn is entranced by the sweetness and light that the Pisces brings to their romance. The Capricorn may even feel inclined to lighten up in the presence of a Pisces lover, and the Pisces may come to enjoy thinking about the down-to-earth pursuits that are dear to the heart of the Capricorn. This makes the romance a miraculous twist of nature, indeed!

258. Aquarius/Aquarius: Do you remember the kid on your block who had the really freaky parents? This kid's parents were the kind of people who thought a fun day at Disney World was more important than homework and encouraged the child to debate his teacher's point of view. This is exactly what you get when two Aquarians enter into a romantic relationship—a lovely, exciting, irresistible adventure. Friends and family will no doubt be envious of and extremely entertained by this wacky duo. Outsiders will admire or be amazed by the freedom and jubilation that Aquarian lovers experience on a daily basis. They may be a constant source of gossip, but this couple of wild and crazy kids will have the time of their lives.

259. **Aquarius/Pisces:** This is a spiritu-
ally charged merger of mind, body,
and soul. The lucky partners in a
Pisces/Aquarius romance can rule
the world—or at least make a differ-
ence while enjoying a highly successful and satisfying life together.
When the energy and daring of the
Aquarius teams up with the boundless creativity of the Pisces, magic
can happen! There's just no under-
estimating the power of a
Pisces/Aquarius romance.

260. **Pisces/Pisces:** Imagine two angels
here on earth having a romantic
relationship among us mere mortal
folk. This pretty much sums up the
Pisces/Pisces romance. Not that
either lover behaves like an angel all
the time. Yet the ever-present theme
of this romance is divine serenity.
These Fish give each other unlimited
permission to dream and live an

ephemeral existence. The only bummer here is that someone is going to have to balance the checkbook!

The Big Getaway:

Romantic Hot Spots around the World

Romance American Style: Love in the City

261. Washington, D.C. is lively and romantic, especially during the springtime. With a lot of passion and a little diplomacy, in Washington, D.C., you and your lover can have an absolutely presidential affair.

262. San Francisco is full of romantic things to do. Take a boat out into the Bay or go to Fisherman's Wharf for a carousel ride. Eat brunch on top of the Fairmont Hotel. Not only will you and your lover taste some of the freshest poached salmon you've ever had, but you will also enjoy spectacular views of the city.

263. If you and your sweetie are high-rollers in love, take a springtime trip to the tackiest romantic city in the world, Las Vegas. Take a romantic helicopter tour over the Grand Canyon or relax in an oversized heart-shaped bathtub back in your hotel's honeymoon suite. You may just find yourselves standing before a velvet-clad justice of the peace in the Elvis chapel!

264. If you both love chocolate, visit Hershey, Pennsylvania. At Hershey's Hotel and Spa in Harrisburg, you and your lover can indulge in decadent spa treatments that include chocolate bubble baths, chocolate mud wraps, and facials.

265. When you visit the Breakers Hotel in Palm Beach, Florida, you and your lover will feel transported into a romantic fairy tale of timeless elegance.

Romance American Style: Town and Country

266. Just an hour and a half north of Los Angeles lies an unspoiled paradise called Santa Barbara. With sweeping views overlooking the Pacific Ocean and fresh salt air, this low-key town is a haven for those who want to escape the smog and fog of Hollywood.

267. Horseback riding is a romantic way to experience a true sense of freedom. If you've never ridden a horse before, you may want to take a lesson or two before galloping off into the wild blue yonder. Take a horseback-riding vacation—a seven-day trek through the green fields of Ireland or up into the romantic hills of Tuscany, or,

closer to home, try a dude ranch in Wyoming or Arizona.

268. Virginia is for lovers. Williamsburg, Virginia, is a lovely little town that has been completely restored to the 1770s. You and your lover can actually experience what it was like to live in George Washington's time. Romantic times, indeed.

269. This fall, put the heart back in your relationship by visiting America's heartland, Indiana. Take a drive through the plains and enjoy an all-American romance. You don't have to travel to a far-away country to enjoy an exotic romantic getaway.

270. Are you and your lover ready for a whole lot of love with a real Western flair? How about moseying on down to Oklahoma? One day in Oklahoma will make you and your lover want to ride off into the blazing sunset, never to be seen again!

271. When you and your lover crave a secluded retreat with all the modern conveniences known to mankind, Fisher Island in Florida is the perfect answer.

Long Island

272. The Hamptons are the most famous place in the United States to spend your summer break. This eastern Long Island locale attracts Wall Streeters, entrepreneurs, designers, and other moguls. The two of you can have the time of your lives in this very unique country setting.

273. Visit Montauk Point in Long Island to see the sun rise. You and your lover will experience true peace and tranquility as you gaze out over this natural harbor.

Love in New England

274. The Berkshire Mountains are perfect for anyone who could use some fresh mountain air. They provide an easily accessible retreat from the hustle and bustle of the real world. No matter how you choose to do it in the Berkshires, you and your lover can enjoy a sexy, secluded time away.

275. Connecticut is an incredibly beautiful and romantic place to visit. It creates the perfect atmosphere for warm, cozy love and intimacy.

276. On the East Coast, the state of Vermont offers great skiing, romantic little inns, and the home of Ben and Jerry's ice cream!

Mi Amor in Mexico

277. Hidden high in the hills above the Atlantic Ocean, on the outskirts of downtown Acapulco, sits Las Brisas, Mexico's gift to lovers of the world. There are no televisions or radios in the room, so this resort is really for lovers who want to get away from it all.

278. Playa del Carmen, Mexico, is fast becoming the place to be on the Mexican Riviera. This is a nonstop party haven with endless cocktails, beach parties, and loud music that plays into the wee hours of the morning. You and your lover can be part of the new emerging international scene as you indulge in a tequila-soaked romance.

279. O, Canada! Canada probably has the most romantic winter getaways on the North American continent, including European castle-like resorts surrounded by breathtaking mountains.

A European Romance

280. What could be more romantic than treating your lover to a trip to Paris? Stroll hand-in-hand by the Seine and spend a cozy night sipping wine.

281. If you need to get the joie de vivre back into your relationship, then take a trip to the irresistibly romantic Loire Valley. Its winding rivers and rolling hills, as well as harvest-time wine tastings, can get anyone in the mood for love!

282. The Netherlands is a perfect place for adventurous lovers. Amsterdam has earned an international reputation for being the capital of uninhibited sexuality. Give each other permission to do things you wouldn't ordinarily do if you were anywhere else!

283. If you are looking for a great getaway off the beaten path, Romania is the place for you. The country has always been a pioneer in the development of spa treatments (long before America was filled with fancy spas). Recapture your strength and youth together and have a red hot Romanian romance!

284. Nestled high in the rocky hills above the calm Mediterranean Sea lies the tiny principality of Monaco, perhaps one of the most romantic spots on earth. No matter what your budget is, you can always find something romantic to experience in Monte Carlo.

285. Tuscany has some of the most lovely and lush landscapes you will ever see. And if that is not enough to entice you, the sweet, pungent aroma of olives and grapes growing all over the countryside will seduce you to no end.

286. If you're ready for an Alpine journey, join the jet-set and European royalty for a visit to Switzerland's most time-honored romantic getaway. You and your lover will leave here with wonderful memories—and a killer recipe for strudel!

287. One very romantic country that is finally getting attention is Iceland. Iceland offers unparalleled natural beauty to the romantic vacationer.

Take a midnight dip in blue-ice hot springs or ride through the mountains on an Icelandic pony.

Unraveling Asia's Mysteries

288. Seoul, South Korea, is the perfect vacation getaway for lovers who favor the out-of-the-ordinary springtime vacation. Treat your lover to a stay at the Shilla Hotel and meander through the extensive sculpture gardens that surround the incredible property.

289. Lovers of all religions will enjoy a historic romantic getaway in the heart of Israel. Whether you visit the Wailing Wall or shop in the Deisengof section of Tel Aviv, a trip to Israel will restore your faith in love and romance. L'chaim!

290. For lovers who want to breathe what has been scientifically proven to be the cleanest air in the world at 14,000 feet above sea level, go on a five-day mystical tour of Tibet. Cleanse body and soul by enjoying the local delicacy, a Szechwan hot pot.

291. Visit Chiva-Som International Health Resort in Hua Hin, Thailand. You will never be able to duplicate this romantic, ethereal holiday.

292. For those lovers who want a romantic vacation for the mind, body, and soul, the Mandarin Oriental Ananda in the Himalayas has it all. If you and your lover are interested in getting in tune with yourselves and each other, a trip to this Indian paradise will give you a unique sense of all-over renewal.

293. Visit the Taj Mahal in India together. Learn about the great love story that inspired the legendary structure. Your love will also be one for the ages if you take this exhilarating, exotic trip.

The United Kingdom

294. Go to Cliveden in Taplow, England. This is where one of the greatest international, aristocratic forbidden romances took place almost a century ago. Each guestroom has an unbelievable view of the rolling English countryside. You and your lover will feel as if you have been transported to another place and time.

295. Go to London together for a trip so fun that you will hardly notice the drizzle. This is the country that gave us Charles and Camilla and many other royal romantic dramas, after all!

296. Attend Royal Ascot in London. Tell them you need a romantic Ascot Hamper made for two. You will be destined to find true love somewhere beneath a big glob of Devonshire cream and scones.

297. If you and your lover are hearty souls who enjoy a winter's walk along a windswept cliff, then the seaside spot of Cornwall, England, is just the place. Walk hand-in-hand as the Atlantic Ocean crashes below you. A night in an old English inn will make your trip all the more romantic.

298. Ireland is a gorgeous place to visit any time of the year, especially in the fall. Spend weekends exploring Celtic castles or fairytale, cobble-stoned, windswept towns along the coast. The countryside of Ireland is a perfect mix of the ancient and modern romance. You and your lover may just find yourselves leaving the land of Eire with a four-leaf clover of love!

299. In Wales, the waves crashing along the cliffs of Ogmor and Porth Cawl are a breathtaking, romantic sight that you will never forget. Take a trip there, and the next time you kiss your lover, he may just turn into a prince!

Tropical Paradise

300. Bermuda is an hour's flight from the Florida coast and is not quite as warm and steamy as the islands of the Caribbean. Bermuda is perfect for lovers who like good service and don't like to feel stranded, but crave a little bit of paradise.

301. Puerto Rico has a sizzling, sexy Latin identity all its own. You and your lover will come back from San Juan with satisfied smiles on both your faces. Olé!

302. Casa de Campo in La Romana has opened its land doors to anyone who wants to live like a king. It is an aristocratic magnet for the elite and a sweet Caribbean escape from mundane reality. Hide under a palm tree behind dark

sunglasses, pretending to escape the paparazzi.

303. If the two of you are looking for a romantic retreat at the ends of the earth, you and your lover will love Langkawi, Penane, Maldives. You and your lover will be secluded in an ancient tropical rainforest surrounded by exotic foliage and wildlife. When you return from the lush hideaway, you will feel refreshed and ready to take on the hectic pace of your everyday lives.

304. The Maruba Resort and Jungle Spa in Maskall Village, Belize, is the perfect modern jungle hideaway for lovers who prefer to be pampered in a neo-primitive environment. It is an authentic tropical rainforest experience.

305. Allow yourselves to get lost in the Mana Lani Bay Hotel and Bungalows on Hawaii's Kohala Coast. You and your lover will feel a million miles away from the hustle and bustle of daily life.

Getaways for Sophisticated Lovers

306. The Grill Room on top of the Hotel De Paris in Monte Carlo is the epitome of a romantic place to share a quiet dinner. On a clear night, they open the rooftop so that you and your lover are covered by a blanket of stars.

307. For lovers who are more serious winers and diners, you can book a trip to California's Napa Valley or Bordeaux, France, for a gourmet tour of the vineyards. See Chapter 3 for our extensive wine list for lovers!

The Great Outdoors:

Finding Romance in Nature

The Pure Waters of Love

308. Romantic River

- Have dinner along the banks of a river.
- Go down to a river or stream with some pieces of torn-up bread. Throw them in the water to symbolize your wrongdoings being washed away.
- Rediscover your childhood innocence by skipping stones in a babbling brook.

309. Love's Deep Lake

- Find a lake and cannonball into the water together.
- Paddle a canoe together. Drift lazily downstream, and be sure to sit side-by-side!
- Feed the swans together on a fresh spring day.

310. The Sands of Love

- Build a sandcastle together. Write your names in the sand.
- Kick off your shoes and walk hand-in-hand along the beach. Splash in the surf!
- Ride horses bareback on the beach.
- Stand at the edge of the sea, exchange tokens, and toss them into the water so you'll always know where they are.

311. Love Your Lawn—and Each Other

If the farm life is just not for you, then you and your lover can still have a wonderful time tending to your own yard. A menial task like mowing the lawn can become romantic when you do it as a team. If you think about it, there is something very sweet about cutting the first grass of the spring season together. You are partaking in a ritual that signifies the season of renewal.

312. Love Is Like Riding a Bicycle...

Go for a bike ride together. This is a physically healthy and romantic thing to do on a fresh spring day. There's nothing like getting your blood pumping as you and your loved one ride bikes in the park, by a lake, or even just through the streets of town. To be really romantic, why not take a whirl on a bicycle built for two? That way, you'll really get to enjoy your teamwork!

313. Anytime, Anyplace

- Lie on the ground and look up at the sky.
- Play outside together.
- Cuddle in a hammock.

314. Let It Snow

- Go cross-country skiing together.
- Go into your closets and collect

your most interesting personal clothing. Head outside to build two "snow lovers" in your likeness!

· Slip your arms around your lover's waist as the two of you slide down a big hill on an old sled or toboggan. Instead of holding onto his ski jacket, slip your hands around his waist, furtively sneaking under his sweater to warm your icy fingers against his warm skin.

315. My Sun Rises and Sets on You

Find out from your local newspaper or television news at what time the sun will rise. Set your alarm clock and go to a beautiful outdoor spot, or enjoy watching the sunrise from the comfort of a spot on your own property.

Love's Open Field

316. To let off steam and stress from the week, find a big, open field and run through it! You can skip together hand-in-hand, stop to pick flowers, or yell and howl with wild abandon. You and your lover may even want to stop and pick clover. You know what they say: make a wish on a four-leaf clover and watch all your romantic dreams come true!

317. If there is a field near you where baby lambs are grazing, you will find that they make great playmates. Run through a field with lambs and watch them run with you.

318. Have a gourmet picnic amid the tall grass and fresh flowers of a meadow. Pack your best silverware and wine glasses, and eat a savory lunch as you inhale the fresh, grassy breeze. Let the warm sun invigorate you both.

Lost in the Woods

319. By the Woods

- Go on a wilderness vacation.
- Make a date to go hiking three or four times per week. Spring is the perfect time to renew your commitment to good health—and each other.
- Ramble through the forest without asking a park ranger for help—half the fun is finding nature's treasures on your own together.

320. The Ultimate Walk in the Woods

If the two of you have some money saved and are looking to commune with nature—and one another—in the ultimate way, plan a section hike or "thru-hike" of a major trail. The Pacific Crest Trail and Appalachian Trail are two of America's longest hiking trails, spanning over 2,000 miles each. By the time you finish your marathon trek through the wilderness (on average, it takes hikers six to nine months to complete either trail), you will have gained a profound, enduring understanding of one another.

Falling for You

321. Rake your fallen leaves into a big pile, then run and jump right in with abandon. Splash around in the dry, crisp leaves and toss handfuls at one another.

322. The autumnal equinox is the official start of autumn. Grab lunch outside at the park, sitting on a city bench or out in the backyard. Enjoy the pleasure of each other's company while soaking up what is left of the sun's rays before winter.

323. Celestial Love
- Watch a meteor shower. Wish on the falling stars.
- Go outside with your lover and look up at the sky. Find the constellations or a shooting star. Take turns making romantic wishes on a star you select. You can even name a star in honor of your love.
- Sleep beneath the stars at your local beach. Let the warm earth be your bed and the stars your blanket as you rest peacefully after making love.

Conquering Nature with Love

324. Go river fishing together. Hand-in-hand, walk right into the water and cast your baited line. When you feel something bite, reel in the fish together. Have a romantic time conquering your catch.

325. Go camping together. Take your time cooking dinner and roasting marshmallows over an open fire while you share funny stories about your childhood camping adventures and mishaps. Needless to say, end the evening by making love under the stars.

326. Go to the top of a mountain and proclaim your love for each other out in the wild. Find a sun-baked rock atop the mountain and have a picnic together. Enjoy the beautiful view together and let the natural world know just how enduring your love is.

327. Our Secret Tree Fort

Building a tree house together can be incredibly romantic. Both of you should share equally in picking out a spot, buying the materials, and building the house. The tree house is supposed to be a secret romantic hideaway, where you can go to escape the world. It is for the two of you to enjoy with a childlike freedom. Whatever activities you and your lover choose to do, your tree house should always be a place of peace, love, and tranquility.

gently together, taking the beautiful lover together and let the entire
world know just how refreshing your
love is.

324. Our Secret Tree House
Building a tree house together can
be incredibly romantic. Both of you
should share equally in picking out a
spot, buying the materials, and
building the house. The tree house
is supposed to be a secret romantic
hideaway, where you can go to
escape the world. It's up to the two of
you to enjoy with childlike freedom. Whatever activities you and
your lover choose to do, your tree
house should always be a place of
peace, love, and tranquility.

Excursions:

Daytime Activities and Short Trips for Lovers

Quiet Activities for the Quaint at Heart

328. Visit a nearby candle factory where you can dip your own candles. Not only will you both enjoy this quiet, relaxing activity, but you can also put the handmade candles to good use when you get home!

329. Try an old-fashioned horse and carriage ride around your local park. From the driver's top hat to the blankets piled high in the back seat, a horse and carriage will transport you and your lover into your own private world.

330. Make arrangements to go on an evening dogsled ride through the woods or an open field. The calm, cold silence of a winter's night has been known to induce secret

snuggling under your parkas. This night out will clear your heads with crisp, fresh air and fill your hearts with natural joy.

331. Taking a hayride is a wonderful way to enjoy an old-fashioned romance. You'll have a wonderful time keeping each other warm in the crisp, fall air with the stars above and the smell of wood smoke in the air.

332. When you don't have time for a long weekend away, a simple drive through the countryside will give you the break that you need. Taking a nice, long drive through the country will help clear your minds—and your hearts for what is truly important in life.

333. This summer, why not stuff a picnic basket full of gourmet goodies, grab a bottle of wine, a big blanket, and a CD player, and head outside for a romantic picnic?

334. Animal Love

Go to a petting zoo together. It is one thing to visit a regular zoo, but it is a different experience to actually touch, hold, pet, and cuddle baby animals. Going to a petting zoo will bring out your desire to be more nurturing and tactile with each other. Being around baby animals helps us get in touch with our instinctual loving feelings. This experience will open up the pathways to a greater, more loving connection.

335. Love's Spectacular Garden

Check out the botanical gardens in your area. Sometimes old estates that have been turned into open-to-the-public museums also have beautifully manicured gardens for the two of you to ramble through. You can count on a quiet and beguiling atmosphere, surrounded by lush blooms and heady fragrances.

Love on the High Seas

336.

Rent a sailboat for the day. Go out into the ocean or just loll around the harbor. If neither of you know how to sail, then take a sailing lesson at least one or two times before you venture out on your own.

337. Go deep-sea fishing together. Just rent a boat with a captain and have him take you to a spot in the ocean where the fish are biting. Pack a lunch and some wine and make a romantic day of it. Later, share stories of your adventure at sea.

338. There is nothing more soothing than a summer sail on a luxury yacht. Treat yourselves right and bring some caviar and champagne. You and your lover will have an absolutely smashing time!

Amusements for Lovers

339. Take a trip to the circus for an afternoon of escapism. Romance has a great chance to bloom under the Big Top. Buy yourselves some peanuts or share a cotton candy.

What could be more fun for lovers than the greatest show on earth?!

340. Go to a parade together. Whether you watch or march, it is an energetic way for you and your lover to regain that special sense of enthusiasm.

341. A fun, romantic summertime activity is to go to a country fair. You can relive your carefree childhood days as you whip around on the Ferris wheel in the romantic moonlight.

For the Love of the Sport

342. Golf is a great game for a bright spring day. Because it is a rather slow sport, you can really savor the time you spend together. You can work as a team as you learn to play.

343. For those of you who like some rough and tumble to get you going on a spring day, have yourselves a ball playing a little one-on-one soccer. The best way to keep a relationship happy and romantic is to get rid of any negative energy before it gets the best of you. The adrenaline you get when you play a contact sport can put you in the mood for love.

344. Often called the sport of kings, you can find a good polo game in many places. Park your car, open the trunk, and enjoy some champagne. At halftime, you and your lover can enjoy stomping divots or walking around the field together.

345. Call your local skating rink and see if they offer a partner's figure-skating class. It is said that both partners in a romantic relationship require a good sense of balance in order to be there

for each other. With ice-skating, you learn to hold each other up physically and emotionally.

All's Fair in Love...

346. Check out a springtime medieval or Renaissance festival. You and your lover can pretend that you are lord and lady as you explore the culture of Old England.

347. Wander aimlessly through a street fair or farmers' market together, which can make your own boring neighborhood come alive with romance.

Love on a Higher Plane

348. You and your lover will get a kick out of spending the afternoon in your local science museum or planetarium. It will remind you that we are all part of a miraculous universe.

349. Spend the weekend attending a spiritual retreat. Whatever your personal beliefs, you and your lover will benefit greatly from a weekend of reflection and heartfelt contemplation. You will come away from the weekend knowing the deeper meaning of two souls that are in love.

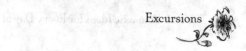

Your Old Teenage Haunts

350. You're Never Too Old To…

- …rent a convertible and kiss in the backseat.
- …buy front-row seats to a hot summer rock concert. Surprise him with backstage passes.
- …go bowling. Bowling is a fun, romantic night out that you and your lover will never outgrow.
- …go to the drive-in. If there is still a drive-in movie theater in your area, this is a perfect place for a romantic interlude.

351. Drive your car to the local make-out spot and relive those teen-dream years. If you don't have a make-out spot, or you are too out-of-it to know where it is, then find any safe, secluded area where you and your lover can have a good time.

Love's Musical Rhythm

352. An old-fashioned American square dance at a lively summer barn is a wonderful getaway. Not only is square dancing a romantic American tradition, but it will also help you get rid of stress or tension.

353. Swing dancing to the big band sounds of the 1940s has made a big comeback. By swinging around the room and enjoying the wonderful music, you and your lover will be transported to a simpler, more innocent, romantic time in our national history.

354. Go country line dancing together. Allow the rhythm to invade your hips and feet and dance circles around one another. The high-energy dancing will create a fun and

playful mood between you and your lover.

355. Short Getaways for Lovers
- Take a romantic train ride.
- Spend a night in the honeymoon suite of a tacky hotel.
- Send your lover to a spa for the weekend.
- Stay in a bed-and-breakfast or cozy inn.

Musical Excursions for Lovers

356. Take your lover to the opera. Allow the poignant music to pierce your hearts and magnify the epic love you have for one another.

357. Go to a karaoke bar. Choose your lover's favorite song and serenade him in front of total strangers. If you are feeling brave, sing a duet together! You may not have perfect pitch, but you will feel in perfect harmony when you sing your hearts out together.

A Lovely Night on the Town

358. Have a candlelit dinner on the roof of a tall building. Enjoy the view— and each other! After a special evening like this, the two of you will feel as if you are on top the world.

359. Have dinner under a river bridge. Listen to the cars pass above you and the water rushing beneath you. Bring a candle and enjoy the gentle breeze from the water and the sparkle in each other's eyes.

360. Treat your lover to a romantic gourmet dinner at a French restaurant. Dress to the nines for one another. Practice your French, the language of love, as you order decadent meals and savor the taste of the food. Pretty soon, you will be feeling l'amour and asking the waiter for your check!

361. After dinner, go out for ice cream at an old-fashioned creamery. Feed one another spoonfuls of the sweet dessert, or take turns licking one another's ice-cream cones. This is a great way to reconnect with your inner child together.

The Love of Shopping

362. Shop for lingerie together. Even if you don't buy anything, the thought of you wearing the skimpy shreds of fabric will be enough to drive your lover wild. Don't get a speeding ticket while rushing home!

363. Visit a pet shop and spend some time with the animals. The purring kittens and whimpering puppies may just inspire the two of you to adopt your first "child"!

364. Have a date in the bookstore. Discuss your favorite volumes and share steaming cups of coffee. Peruse the bookshelves and stop to read romantic poetry or favorite passages to one another. If you are feeling adventurous, head over to

the sexuality section and get some ideas for when you go home later.

365. Go to a video store and stock up on romantic films for a rainy day. As you peruse the shelves, recite favorite lines or scenes to one another. This is a sure way to set a romantic tone for the rest of the day—and your lives!

Best Romantic Ideas

Best Romantic Ideas

_____

_____

_____

_____

_____

_____

_____

_____

_____

_____

Best Romantic Ideas

Best Romantic Ideas

Best Romantic Ideas